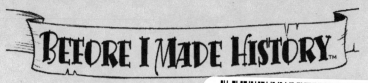

BEFORE I MADE HISTORY™

SEW WHAT, BETSY ROSS?

BY PETER AND CONNIE ROOP

SCHOLASTIC INC.

New York   Toronto   London   Auckland   Sydney
Mexico City   New Delhi   Hong Kong   Buenos Aires

ISBN 0-439-43925-6

Text copyright © 2002 by Peter Roop and Connie Roop.
Illustrations copyright © 2002 by Scholastic Inc.

12 11 10 9 8 7 6 5 4 3 2 1   2 3 4 5 6 7/0

Printed in the U.S.A.   40
First printing, October 2002

*For all of the wonderful young authors
at Poqounock Elementary School,
who inspired me so much!
Keep the writing lights burning!*

Table of Contents

INTRODUCTION

Betsy Ross is famous. She made American flags.

Did you know Betsy Ross also made curtains, quilts, clothes, and blankets?

Betsy Ross was paid to make American flags. Did she really make the first American flag?

The first flags had thirteen stars and thirteen stripes. Did you know each time a new state was added to the flag a new star was added?

Betsy Ross ran her own upholstery business. How did she do this at a time when very few women owned businesses?

Betsy Ross was married three times. Did

you know her real name was Elizabeth Griscom Ross Ashburn Claypoole?

Betsy Ross talked with George Washington. Did you know she sat behind him in church?

Betsy Ross had seven daughters. Did you know she had thirteen brothers and sisters?

Betsy Ross told her story about making the first American flag only to her family. Then how did so many people learn her American flag story?

The answers to these questions lie in who Betsy Ross was as a girl and as a young woman. This book is about Betsy Ross before she made history.

1

BETSY IS BORN

January 1, 1752, was cold, but the sun shone brightly. This was the first day of the first month of a brand-new year. A baby cried. She had just been born at home. Her tired mother held the baby, and the baby stopped crying. The baby was Samuel and Rebecca Griscom's eighth child. They named her Elizabeth. Her family called her by her nickname, Betsy.

Betsy had five big sisters to play with. Later, Betsy had eight little brothers and sisters to play with. The Griscom house was very busy, noisy, and crowded! A large family was common during Betsy's lifetime.

Unfortunately, not every child lived to be an adult. Many children died from yellow

fever, smallpox, measles, whooping cough, and other illnesses. Accidents also claimed many lives. Children drowned. Houses burned. Boats sank. Only nine Griscom children lived to be adults—one boy and eight girls. Fortunately, Betsy survived.

Betsy was born in Philadelphia. Philadelphia was the biggest city in the colony of Pennsylvania. Almost twenty thousand people lived there. Philadelphia was the biggest city in all the thirteen colonies. The first settlers in Philadelphia liked the many trees they found there. They named the streets Pine, Walnut, Spruce, Locust, and Chestnut. To remember the street names, people said this rhyme:

High, Mulberry, Sassafras, Vine,
Chestnut, Walnut, Spruce, and Pine.

Betsy Griscom probably learned this rhyme to find her way around town.

Betsy's father, Samuel Griscom, was a carpenter. He was also a builder. His father and grandfather had built many buildings in Philadelphia. Samuel built houses. He built churches. He built shops. Samuel was a very busy carpenter. He was very busy with his big family, too.

In 1751, Samuel helped build the first tower on the Pennsylvania State House. Today, we call this famous building Independence Hall. Samuel also helped build the Friends, or Quaker, Meeting House. This is where Betsy and her family worshiped.

Betsy's family were devout Quakers. Quakers tried to live simple, peaceful lives. They dressed in plain clothes. They worked hard in their homes, shops, and schools. Quakers had many strict rules. One was that Quakers could only marry Quakers. Another was that Quakers could not fight in wars.

Samuel Griscom also helped build Carpenters' Hall. At first, this was a special building just for carpenters. Later, many meetings were held in the hall. Benjamin Franklin even had a library in Carpenters'

Hall. Samuel was so important that his name was written on a wall in Carpenters' Hall.

Samuel Griscom's talented hands helped build many other buildings in Philadelphia. These sturdy buildings had thick brick walls. They had strong oak beams. Some of the buildings Betsy's father built still stand in Philadelphia today.

2
BUSY BETSY

On the day Betsy was born, there was no United States. Instead, there were thirteen colonies owned by England. Betsy lived in the colony of Pennsylvania. There were twelve other colonies besides Pennsylvania. They were Massachusetts, New Hampshire, New York, Connecticut, Rhode Island, New Jersey, Delaware, Maryland, Virginia, North Carolina, South Carolina, and Georgia.

When Betsy was born, Philadelphia was the busiest city in the American colonies. Ships from England landed at the docks. Farmers from the country came into town in their loaded wagons. They sold wool, chickens, ducks, geese, pigs, wood, brooms, meat, eggs, vegetables, fruits, and cheese. The farmers bought cloth, glass, pots, pans, needles, thread, tea, coffee, sugar, salt, tools, and many more things in Philadelphia's busy shops.

Philadelphia was in the middle of the thirteen colonies. It was easy to sail to the ocean from Philadelphia. The city was important to the other colonies. Here, they traded for what they needed. Wheat, wood, flour, and other American products were shipped to England. Cotton cloth, iron, paper, pottery, sugar, silk, books, guns, and linen were shipped to Philadelphia.

Betsy Griscom grew up in the busy, bustling city of Philadelphia. Young girls like Betsy learned the skills to be good housekeepers and mothers. As soon as they were old enough, they helped with cooking, washing, cleaning, gardening, and sewing. Girls also helped take care of their younger sisters and brothers. Few girls learned a trade outside their homes.

Starting at age five, young Betsy did chores. She learned by watching her family.

She watched her mother and sisters chop vegetables, cut meat, and bake bread. When Betsy was old enough, she helped cook over the blazing fire in the kitchen.

Betsy helped wash the dishes. She carried water from the well. After the water was heated, the dishes were washed and dried. Betsy's brothers kept the wood box filled. While Betsy worked inside, she heard them chopping wood outside. Every day, the many beds had to be made and the floors swept. Each week, the clothes had to be washed. After they were clean, the clothes had to be ironed with heavy, hot irons.

In the spring, Betsy helped plant carrots, onions, potatoes, and cabbage in her family's garden. In the summer, Betsy pulled weeds and carried water to the growing plants. In the fall, Betsy helped harvest the garden. She picked and cleaned vegetables. She carried them to the cellar to be stored for the winter.

But best of all, Betsy liked making clothes. The Griscoms did not buy new clothes. They made their shirts, skirts, aprons, bonnets, pants, blouses, underwear, and stockings by hand.

Mrs. Griscom bought wool from the farmers. Betsy and her sisters would card the wool. Carding took out tangles and straightened the wool. Carding was hard work for Betsy's small hands.

The wool was twisted into long strings. Betsy's mother spun the wool on her spinning wheel. Betsy enjoyed watching the spinning wheel go round and round. Her mother's skillful fingers held the wool strings tight.

Soon, long, strong threads came off the spinning wheel. Betsy and her sisters wound the thread onto spools. The thread was woven into cloth. The cloth was dyed white, gray, or brown. The cloth was cut and sewed to make new clothes for the whole family. With fourteen children and two adults, many clothes had to be made.

Betsy especially liked cutting and sewing the cloth. She learned how to thread a needle and sew. Sometimes, Betsy pricked her finger

with a needle. Her finger was too small for a thimble. But Betsy was careful not to let a drop of blood stain the cloth. Betsy hoped to be an excellent seamstress someday, like her mother.

Betsy's clothes were very simple. Quakers like Betsy's family lived simple lives. Betsy's dresses were gray. Her apron was white. Her stockings were white. Betsy wore a white bonnet on her head when she went outside. Betsy's mother and sisters dressed the same way. Betsy's father and brothers also dressed in plain clothes.

The furniture in Betsy's house was simple, too. Betsy's father made the tables, chairs, and beds out of wood. The furniture was sturdy and strong, but it was not decorated.

Betsy's parents set good examples for their children. Betsy's mother worked hard at home. Her father worked hard building. They saved their money. They went to meeting (church) two times a week. They read the Bible every day. And they loved their family very much.

3

BETSY GOES TO SCHOOL

Betsy's family did not play games, listen to music, or dance. Good Quakers did not do these things. Betsy's family were good Quakers.

Reading was important in Betsy's family. All the Griscom children learned how to read. They read the Bible—Quakers rarely read other books. But Betsy also had fun with her family. They talked and laughed while they did their many chores. They told stories. They walked in Philadelphia's many parks. Sometimes, they took a boat ride on the Delaware River. Betsy's family went on picnics. In the winter, they went sledding and skated on the frozen river. They played chase and had snowball fights.

One day, Betsy's life changed. She was very excited. She had watched her big sisters and brothers go to school six days a week. She had wished she could go to school, too! Finally, when she was six years old, Betsy's wish came true.

When Betsy was young, few girls went to school. But the Griscoms wanted all their children to learn how to read, write, and count. School was very important to Betsy's family.

Betsy was excited on her first day of school. Now she could learn how to read, write, and do arithmetic like her big sisters and brothers. She would still have to do her chores at home. Her days would be even busier. But Betsy was full of energy. She did not mind the extra work.

Betsy walked proudly to the home of Rebecca Jones. This was to be her first school. Mrs. Jones's school was a few blocks from Betsy's home. Mrs. Jones was firm with her students. They did what she told them. Betsy did what Mrs. Jones said. Mrs. Jones was just

like Betsy's mother. Betsy enjoyed learning to read, write, and count. But she especially liked sewing time. Her hand did not wiggle so much now when she threaded the needle. She was careful not to prick her fingers with the sharp needle. Finally, her finger was big enough for the thimble!

Some of Betsy's stitches were not very straight. Sometimes, she did not pull the end of the thread tight enough. But Betsy did not give up. Each day, she got better and better. Betsy sewed things her family needed. She made baby clothes for her younger brothers and sisters. She sewed patches of cloth together to make quilts for their beds.

By age eight, Betsy was too old for Mrs. Jones's school. Betsy was even more excited. Now she could go to the real school with bigger girls and boys. She could go to the Quaker Friends School! Friends School was a Quaker school, but children who were not Quakers went there, too. Betsy was happy because now she could make new friends.

Betsy's new school was near the redbrick

State House. Every day Betsy looked up to see the tower her father had helped build. She looked at Carpenters' Hall, which her grandfather and father had helped build. Most of the time Betsy enjoyed Friends School. The schoolmaster was very strict. Everyone obeyed his rules. When a child broke a rule, he or she was punished on Saturday morning. The schoolmaster took his thick switch and spanked the naughty child. The switch stung like a bee. Betsy never wanted to feel the switch's sting!

Betsy was cheerful and friendly. She soon made new friends. Her best friend was Susan Claypoole. Betsy and Susan laughed, talked, and played together. Betsy had fun with Susan's brother John, too.

Betsy's days were busier than ever before. After she did her morning chores, Betsy walked to school. When the big bell in the State House tower rang at eight o'clock, Betsy was sitting straight in her seat. From eight to ten o'clock, Betsy studied. She practiced her letters. Betsy dipped her feather pen into the ink and carefully wrote her letters and numbers.

There were not many books when Betsy was growing up, so Betsy read from a special kind of book called a hornbook. A hornbook was shaped like a paddle. Letters and words were written on a piece of paper. The paper was covered with a thin sheet of horn. The horn was so thin Betsy could read through it. Betsy also read the Bible. Betsy did not read storybooks at school. None of the Quaker children did.

Betsy learned math, too. She learned how to add, subtract, multiply, and divide. Many Quaker families ran shops. Betsy learned how to keep the record books for a shop, too.

The last two hours in the morning were Betsy's favorite. This was when the students chose something they loved to do. They picked a skill they might use someday to earn a living. Some boys made toy furniture from wood. They planned to be carpenters.

Some boys practiced math. They hoped to be clerks in shops. Others made brooms, spoons, or wooden plates. They would need to make these things for their own homes someday. Betsy, of course, picked sewing.

4
BETSY IS THE BEST

Soon Betsy's fingers were long and strong. She practiced making perfect stitches in her sampler. A sampler was a piece of cloth on which a girl practiced her sewing skills. She would stitch numbers, letters, and sentences. As her skills got better, she would sew pictures of animals and plants. Betsy sewed her ABC's. When she was good enough, Betsy sewed a sentence from the Bible. Here is a verse Betsy may have stitched on one of her many samplers:

This is my Sampler,
Here you see
What care my Mother
Took of me.

Betsy sewed pictures of houses. She sewed Bible animals like lions, sheep, and doves. She sewed numbers. When Betsy finished a sampler, she stitched in the date. Betsy made each sampler better and better. Betsy's stitches grew tighter and straighter. Her knots were stronger. Betsy had names for the many different stitches she learned. She stitched a fernstitch, a finnystitch, a chainstitch, a fisherstitch, a whipstitch, a crossstitch, and even a mousestitch.

At noon, Betsy ran home for dinner. She helped her mother set the table. After she ate, Betsy helped clean up before walking back to school. Betsy spent the next two hours studying. Then she returned to her sewing. Betsy never seemed to get tired of her needle and thread.

Betsy sewed at home, too. Her great-aunt Sarah now lived with Betsy's family. Great-aunt Sarah helped cook and clean for the large Griscom family. She helped take care of Betsy's younger sisters and brothers.

Just like Betsy, Great-aunt Sarah loved to

sew. Great-aunt Sarah once ran her own business. This was unusual because during this time, men ran most businesses. Great-aunt Sarah had sewed clothes for wealthy women. She had stitched underwear, bonnets, blouses, and skirts. Great-aunt Sarah liked her many customers. But she could also get angry. One day, a man would not pay his bill. Great-aunt Sarah put his name in the newspaper. Putting someone's name in the newspaper was common, especially if that person did not pay his or her bills. The embarrassed man quickly paid Great-aunt Sarah what he owed her!

Betsy enjoyed being with Great-aunt Sarah. She liked watching Great-aunt Sarah's fast fingers. Her needle quickly darted up and down. Her stitches were straight and even. She never pricked her fingers. Betsy hoped someday she would be as good a seamstress as Great-aunt Sarah.

One day, Friends School had a show. The students displayed their best work. There were carved toys, neat notebooks, and beautiful samplers. Betsy was nervous. Her sampler was displayed with the others. Parents and friends looked at the samplers. They talked about the straight stitches and tight knots. They enjoyed the special designs.

Many people stared at Betsy's sampler. She was pleased when they nodded and smiled. Betsy was surprised! Her sampler was picked as one of the best! Betsy's hard work was paying off. Her dream of becoming an excellent seamstress was coming true! Could she even dream of one day owning a shop like Great-aunt Sarah?

5
BETSY LEAVES SCHOOL

In 1762, when Betsy was ten years old, three thousand people in Philadelphia died from yellow fever. Many people moved out of town. The Griscoms stayed. But Betsy did not get sick.

In 1763, Betsy had another surprise. One day, the earth began to shake and quake. Dishes rattled. Windows broke. Chimneys fell. An earthquake hit Philadelphia! No one in Betsy's family was hurt. But Betsy had extra work to do to clean up the mess.

On January 1, 1764, Betsy turned twelve years old. Philadelphia was busier than ever before. Hundreds of ships sailed to the Philadelphia docks. Dozens of ships were being built, too. Sail makers cut and stitched great canvas sails. Rope makers twisted miles of new rope. All these ships carried products in and out of Philadelphia. Many ship captains, merchants, and shopkeepers grew rich.

More money meant more people could afford to buy expensive things. More books and fancy foods were sold. More people bought fine upholstered furniture. They bought linen and lace tablecloths. They paid for rich, thick carpets.

One day, Betsy went into John Webster's Upholstery Shop. Betsy enjoyed his shop. She saw beautiful new cloth from England, France, Ireland, and even China. Betsy watched workers making curtains, blankets, umbrellas, mattresses, tents, tablecloths, and flags. Betsy wondered what it would be like to work in such a marvelous shop.

One day, Betsy saw a young girl struggling with her work. Her stitches were not strong and straight. The blanket would quickly fall apart. Betsy waited before saying a word. She did not want to make anyone angry. But Betsy could not stand by and watch someone

do a poor sewing job! Betsy finally got up the courage to say something.

Betsy told the girl what she was doing wrong. She showed her how to make straighter, stronger stitches. John Webster, the shop owner, listened to what Betsy had to say. Betsy was right. Now the seamstress knew just what to do.

Betsy's father was very busy. People wanted new houses. New churches were also being built. Mr. Griscom was building all the time. But Mr. Griscom was also a good Quaker. He was thrifty. He did not spend his hard-earned money on fancy things. Besides, he had little money to spare. He had just finished building a new home for his family on Arch Street. Betsy's father could no longer afford to send Betsy to Friends School. Betsy had had her turn at school. Now it was time for her younger brothers and sisters to go to school.

Betsy was sad. She would miss Friends School. She had learned so much there. She would also miss seeing her friends Susan and

John Claypoole. Betsy hoped she might have time to see them when school was out.

But Betsy was excited, too. Her father decided Betsy needed to use her sewing skills in a different way. He did not want her to keep making samplers and clothes. Mr. Griscom believed Betsy should learn a trade. He wanted Betsy to become an apprentice in an upholstery shop. There Betsy would sew fine cloth onto furniture. She would make special carpets. She would stitch fancy tablecloths. She would sew nice curtains. She would cover umbrellas with silk. She would use her sewing skills to decorate whole rooms.

Betsy was excited. If she learned the upholstery trade, she knew she could always find work. Someday, maybe her dream of owning her own shop might come true.

Few girls, however, learned a trade in those days. Most girls were expected to get married and take care of their home. Betsy's family had a different idea. Betsy was so good at sewing that her parents believed she should use her special talent with a needle and thread outside their home. Apprentices usually worked for someone for five or six years while learning a skill or a trade. The master taught the apprentice the skill. The master also gave the apprentice a place to live and fed him or her, too. The apprentice did not get paid.

Apprentices learned carpentry, shipbuilding, glassblowing, bricklaying, cabinet- and furniture-making, blacksmithing, and many other skilled trades. A hardworking apprentice hoped to open his or her own shop someday.

Betsy's father took her to John Webster's Upholstery Shop. Betsy was scared. This was the same shop where she had corrected the worker! Mr. Webster was happy to see Betsy again. He knew she was skilled with a needle and thread. When Betsy's father asked if she could apprentice in his shop, Mr. Webster said yes! Betsy was thrilled. She could hardly wait to begin work in a real shop.

6

BETSY'S FIRST JOB

Betsy was disappointed during her first days at the upholstery shop. She did not sew fancy tablecloths. She did not stitch fine linen. Instead, Betsy ran many errands. She swept the floor and sprinkled sand at the front door to keep down the dust. She climbed down the steep steps to the cellar to get yards of heavy material. Betsy took sharp needles to the seamstresses. She carried canvas straps, brass nails, and chair stuffings to other workers. When someone needed something, they called, "Betsy!"

Betsy learned that a beginning apprentice had the worst jobs. But Betsy was used to working hard and doing her chores. Still, her eager fingers itched to stitch the beautiful fabrics she carried.

Mr. Webster watched Betsy. He saw how willingly she did her jobs. One day he asked Betsy to cut out some patterns. Betsy picked up her scissors. She must not make a mistake. She took a deep breath. Slowly and carefully, she cut the cloth. She cut so well that soon Mr. Webster gave her other sewing jobs to do.

For the first time in her life, Betsy cut smooth silk for umbrellas. She cut light linen for tablecloths. She made blankets. She cut and sewed curtains for beds. She made mattresses and drapes. Betsy even made flags. The hundreds of ships coming to Philadelphia needed new flags to replace those that were worn out.

Betsy's sewing skills improved. The skills she had learned at home and at school made her one of the best apprentices. Betsy worked hard every day, and she really enjoyed it.

Betsy had always been friendly. Her blue eyes sparkled as she sewed. One of her new friends was another apprentice named John Ross. John's father was a minister at Christ Church. For many people, Christ Church was the most important church in Philadelphia. Its steeple towered above the city.

Christ Church was not a Quaker place of worship. Christ Church belonged to the Church of England. John's father wanted him to be a minister. But that was not John's dream. He had always enjoyed making things with his hands. He liked fixing furniture. He liked covering chairs with material. John dreamed of owning his own upholstery shop someday. Against his father's wishes, John Ross became an apprentice at John Webster's Upholstery Shop.

Betsy and John became good friends. John was tall and handsome. Betsy liked John's laugh. She liked his willingness to help others. Betsy admired his skilled hands as they worked. John also knew how to run a busi-

ness. Betsy hoped his dream of owning his own shop would come true.

John liked Betsy, too. He liked her brown hair and dancing blue eyes. He admired her skilled fingers as they cut, stitched, and sewed. John especially enjoyed Betsy's quiet confidence. Betsy told John about her dream of owning her own upholstery shop. John shared this dream, too!

With so much in common, Betsy Griscom and John Ross fell in love. They decided to get married. There was a big problem, however. Betsy was a Quaker. John belonged to the Church of England. Betsy and John knew that their parents would not let them get married.

So they made a plan. They would run away, get married, come back, and someday together open their own upholstery shop.

7
BETSY BECOMES BETSY ROSS

Betsy and John made their plan. They did not tell their parents. They waited until Betsy was twenty-one years old. Then her parents could not stop her from marrying John.

On Thursday, November 4, 1773, Betsy and John were unusually busy at the shop. They took even more care with their work. They finished all the jobs Mr. Webster had given them. They did not want to disappoint Mr. Webster. He had been a good master to them. He had taught them how to run a fine upholstery shop.

That night Betsy and John left Philadelphia. They walked down to the Delaware River. A cold wind blew hard. Betsy and John climbed into a small rowboat. John rowed across the mile-wide river in the dark until they reached the New Jersey shore. Their friend, William Hugg, met Betsy and John. William found a justice of the peace to marry them. Finally, they were Betsy and John Ross.

One family story tells of Betsy and John being married in front of a huge fireplace. The fire burned brightly. Beside the fireplace stood a tall grandfather clock that was missing one hand. The clock is no longer there. But the same big stone fireplace still warms people in Gloucester, New Jersey.

Betsy and John were very happy. One of their dreams had come true. They were married. Now they had to return to Philadelphia and face their parents. Betsy's parents were very angry when they learned that Betsy had married John. They told Betsy she could no longer be a Quaker because it was against Quaker rules for her to marry someone who was not a Quaker.

Betsy loved John. She shared his dreams. Betsy stopped being a Quaker and joined John at Christ Church. Betsy and John worshiped

at Christ Church for many years. Today, Betsy's pew is marked with her name. A small American flag hangs by it. Just in front of Betsy's pew is the place where George Washington worshiped when he was in Philadelphia.

Mr. Webster was not surprised that Betsy and John had gotten married. He did not want to lose these two excellent workers, so he hired Betsy and John to keep working in his shop. Betsy and John were now paid for their hard work. With the money, they soon opened their own shop.

First, they bought John his own set of upholstery tools. Now he had the hammers, awls, and pliers he needed to do his work. Then they bought Betsy the best needles, thread, and scissors they could afford.

Betsy had always admired the beautiful cloth from England. But there was trouble brewing between England and the thirteen American colonies. The English thought they should be able to make Americans pay taxes. The Americans said that the English could not make them pay taxes. They felt that only American colonists could tax American colonists.

In 1773, the year Betsy and John were married, King George III grew angry with the Americans. He made up his mind. The American colonies would pay a tax on tea whether they liked it or not.

The Americans did not like it at all! The thirteen colonies joined together against England. They stopped buying tea from the English. Instead, they made "Liberty Tea" from roots and plants. Betsy drank Liberty Tea even though it was not as tasty as English tea. The colonists sent a strong message to England.

King George did not like this strong message. He could be just as stubborn as the Americans. King George demanded that they drink English tea and pay his tax.

One day, a ship loaded with tea sailed into Boston. American patriots refused to unload the English tea. Instead, they dumped 342 chests of tea into the water.

King George was angrier than ever when he heard about this "Boston Tea Party." He sent ships and soldiers to take over Boston. When Betsy and John heard about the Boston Tea Party, they thought it was a good idea. So did many other people in Philadelphia.

On December 27, 1773, the bell in the State House tower rang across Philadelphia. More than eight thousand people gathered and cheered for the people of Boston. Betsy and John Ross were American patriots and were probably in the huge crowd.

8

Betsy and John
Open Their Shop

In the summer of 1774, men from all thirteen colonies came to Philadelphia to make plans to fight against King George. The men called themselves the Continental Congress. Betsy was proud because the Congress met in Carpenters' Hall, which her father and grandfather had helped build.

People in all thirteen colonies, including John and Betsy, felt united as Americans. By 1775, Americans wanted independence from England. They did not want the English telling them what to do. They wanted to make their own decisions.

Betsy and John felt this way, too. They also wanted their independence. They liked

Mr. Webster. He had been good to them. But they still dreamed of owning their own shop.

In the summer of 1775, America had not yet declared its independence from England. But Betsy and John decided to declare their independence. They told Mr. Webster they were going to open their own shop. He was sad to see them leave. He wished them good luck. He knew they would need it. Running an upholstery shop was hard.

Betsy and John moved to a small brick building on Arch Street. They lived upstairs. In the front room downstairs, Betsy and John opened their upholstery shop. Their dream had finally come true! They hung a sign outside. The sign read JOHN ROSS, UPHOLSTERER. History does not tell us why Betsy's name was not on the sign. But Betsy was John's partner. She talked to customers. She took orders. She sewed curtains, mattresses, and tablecloths. She showed off the fine fabrics they had in their shop. Whenever she could, Betsy sewed flags for ships. But with war

coming with England, not so many ships came to Philadelphia anymore.

Betsy and John worked hard six days a week in their shop. They opened early and closed late. On Sundays, they rested. They went to Christ Church. They walked and talked. They visited friends. They enjoyed being together.

The argument between England and America grew worse. Betsy joined a group called "the Fighting Quakers." They made uniforms for American soldiers. They knitted socks. They made knapsacks. Betsy was no longer a Quaker, but many of her friends still were. Betsy wanted to help them.

John wanted to help American patriots, too. He joined the local militia, which was like a small army. In the militia, John marched, drilled, and prepared to fight when General George Washington needed him. While he waited, John was given an important job. He was picked to guard a supply of very valuable guns, gunpowder, and cannons.

January 1, 1776, arrived. It was Betsy's

twenty-fourth birthday. She and John cele-
brated quietly above the Ross Upholstery
Shop. That same day, a new flag called the
Continental Colors was raised near Boston.
General Washington had wanted a new flag
to fly for his new American army on New
Year's Day. The Continental Colors flag had
thirteen red and white stripes. The red and
white stripes stood for the thirteen American
colonies. In the top left-hand corner, there
was a small English flag. This was to show
that the colonies were still ruled by England.
That day, Betsy had no idea how important
American flags would someday be to her.

While John worked in the army, Betsy ran
the shop on her own. She took orders. She
sold fabrics. She made things. She kept good
business records. Betsy liked running the
Ross Upholstery Shop.

9

BETSY MAKES A FLAG

One cold January day, John proudly put on the uniform that Betsy had made for him. He marched off to guard the gunpowder.

Later that day, Betsy heard a knock on the shop door. She hoped it was a new customer. A group of army men stood on her doorstep. They carried a wounded man. The wounded man was Betsy's husband. The men carried John upstairs. They told Betsy that the gunpowder had exploded. John had been caught in the blast and was severely wounded.

Betsy nursed John. She cleaned his wounds, fed him, and talked to him. But John's wounds were very bad. Soon, John Ross died. John Ross was buried in the cemetery of Christ Church.

After the funeral, Betsy walked home. She was only twenty-four years old, and she was now a widow. Betsy Ross was alone in the world. Betsy wondered what she should do. She could return to her parents. No, Betsy decided. Should she sell the upholstery shop and go back to work for Mr. Webster? No, Betsy decided. The shop was her dream. It had been John's dream, too.

Alone at home, Betsy made her decision. She would keep the shop open. She would run it herself. Great-aunt Sarah had run her business. Betsy Ross could, too. The thirteen United States were fighting for their independence. Betsy would fight for her independence, too!

Betsy hung up a new sign in her shop window: ELIZABETH ROSS, UPHOLSTERER. Betsy put samples of her work in the window. People looked in and saw a very busy Betsy Ross.

But keeping the shop open was difficult. A war was coming, and people did not want to spend money on fine linens, carpets, and bedspreads. Betsy spent more time making clothes. Betsy made shirts for American officers. She even made shirts for General Washington. But it wasn't enough. Betsy worried that she might have to close her shop. She needed steady business.

One day, three men knocked on Betsy's door. One man was John's uncle, Colonel George Ross. The other two men were Robert Morris and General George Washington. Betsy invited them into her shop. She led them to the back parlor, the best room in her house.

The three men wanted an American flag. They asked Betsy if she could make one. Betsy said, "I do not know. I will try."

The gentlemen wanted a flag like the Continental Colors that General Washington had flown over Boston. The flag had to have thirteen stripes and thirteen stars. But it would not have the hated English flag in the corner.

General Washington spread a drawing of the flag on Betsy's table. Betsy saw that the flag was too square. She said the flag should

be wider and longer so it would wave better in the wind.

General Washington gave Betsy a pattern for the stars he wanted. Betsy looked at the pattern. The stars had six points. Betsy said that the stars should have only five points. Betsy folded a piece of paper. With a quick snip of her sharp scissors, she cut out a star with five points. The men were pleased. The American flag would have stars with only five points.

But Betsy wasn't the only seamstress the men visited.

Betsy worried whether she would get the job of making the flags. If she did, then she could keep her shop open. If she didn't, she did not know what she would do.

Betsy went right to work. She cut out seven red stripes. She cut out six white stripes. She cut out thirteen stars. She cut out a blue square. Betsy sewed the stars onto the blue square. She stitched the thirteen stripes together. She sewed the star-filled blue square in the upper left-hand corner.

Betsy took her new flag to the committee. She went with the men down to the docks on the river. Betsy's flag was raised to the top of a ship's mast. The wind blew. The star-spangled banner fluttered. Everyone agreed. Betsy's flag was the best!

10

BETSY MAKES FLAGS
FOR THE REST OF HER LIFE

Betsy began making flags for the American navy. She made flags for American merchant ships, too. She made flags for the American army. Betsy Ross made flags for the rest of her long life.

Betsy got married again. On June 15, 1777, Betsy married Captain Joseph Ashburn. Betsy and Joseph lived at Betsy's home on Arch Street. Betsy kept her upholstery shop open. She sewed more flags. Here Betsy had her first two daughters.

Then Joseph died in the war with England. Betsy was on her own again. Betsy's childhood friend John Claypoole brought her the sad news about Joseph's death.

Soon Betsy and John fell in love and were married. Betsy was now Betsy Griscom Ross Ashburn Claypoole. Betsy and John had five daughters. All the while, Betsy ran her business. She kept making American flags.

When her daughters were old enough, Betsy taught them how to sew. Soon the girls were helping their mother make flags.

John Claypoole died in 1817. Betsy was sixty-five years old. But she kept working in her shop.

Betsy finally stopped sewing when her eyes got bad. She retired in 1827 when she was seventy-five years old.

Now Betsy had more time to enjoy her grandchildren. She liked to sit in her rocking chair and tell them stories about her life. Her favorite story was about when General Washington asked her to make the first flag of the United States of America.

Betsy died on January 30, 1836. She was eighty-four years old.

During Betsy's life there were many changes. The new nation of the United States

was born. Seven presidents were elected. Betsy had sewed thirteen stars on the first flag. When she died, there were twenty-five stars on the flag. Twelve more states had joined the United States.

Betsy was buried at her Arch Street home. An American flag flies by Betsy's grave all day and all night.

Who would have guessed Betsy's role in American history when she was born on that cold January day in 1752?